To all those who work with earth to supply our Earth with food—R. M.

Also in this series:

Ralph Masiello's Ancient Egypt Drawing Book
Ralph Masiello's Bug Drawing Book
Ralph Masiello's Dinosaur Drawing Book
Ralph Masiello's Dragon Drawing Book
Ralph Masiello's Ocean Drawing Book
Ralph Masiello's Robot Drawing Book

Other books illustrated by Ralph Masiello:

The Dinosaur Alphabet Book
The Extinct Alphabet Book
The Flag We Love
The Frog Alphabet Book
The Icky Bug Alphabet Book
The Icky Bug Counting Book
The Mystic Phyles: Beasts
The Skull Alphabet Book
The Yucky Reptile Alphabet Book
Cuenta los insectos

Copyright © 2012 by Ralph Masiello
All rights reserved, including the right of reproduction in whole or in part in any form. Charlesbridge and colophon are registered trademarks of Charlesbridge Publishing, Inc.

Published by Charlesbridge
85 Main Street
Watertown, MA 02472
(617) 926-0329
www.charlesbridge.com

Library of Congress Cataloging-in-Publication Data
Masiello, Ralph.
    Ralph Masiello's farm drawing book / Ralph Masiello.
        p. cm.
    ISBN 978-1-57091-537-6 (reinforced for library use)
    ISBN 978-1-57091-538-3 (softcover)
1. Domestic animals in art—Juvenile literature. 2. Livestock in art—Juvenile literature. 3. Drawing—Technique—Juvenile literature. I. Title.
NC783.8.D65M37 2012
743.6—dc22   2011004024

Printed in China
(hc) 10 9 8 7 6 5 4 3 2 1
(sc) 10 9 8 7 6 5 4 3 2 1

Illustrations done in mixed media
Display type set in Couchlover, designed by Chank, Minneapolis, Minnesota;
    text type set in Goudy
Color separations by KHL Chroma Graphics, Singapore
Printed and bound September 2011 by Jade Productions
    in Heyuan, Guangdong, China
Production supervision by Brian G. Walker
Designed by Susan Mallory Sherman and Martha MacLeod Sikkema

Howdy, Fellow Artists!

This is Farmer Ralph, welcoming you to my book on how to draw things found on a farm. I have great admiration for farmers. They are tough, hard-working folks who tend and grow all kinds of things that we need to live. Without farmers and farms, where would our food come from?

In this book I will show you simple ways to draw common barnyard animals. You'll also learn how to draw hay bales, a tractor, a farmer, and a barn.

Carefully follow the steps in red to create your own farm drawings. Use the challenge steps in blue to add more character and detail. And remember . . . have fun!

Ralph

Choose your tools

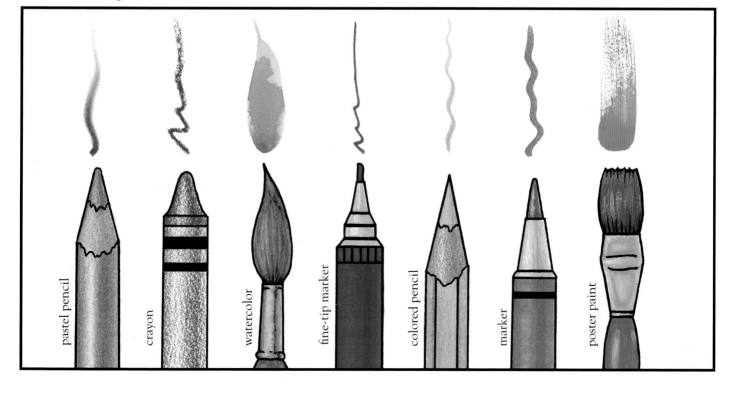

pastel pencil | crayon | watercolor | fine-tip marker | colored pencil | marker | poster paint

Baby Chicks

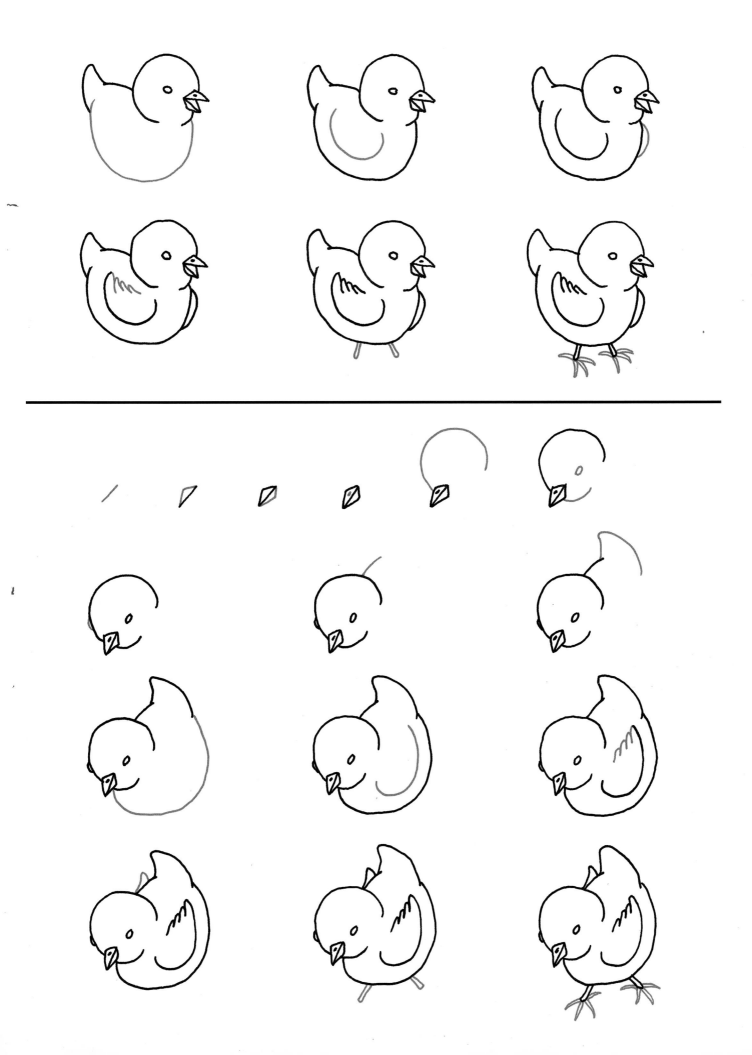

Hen

Rooster

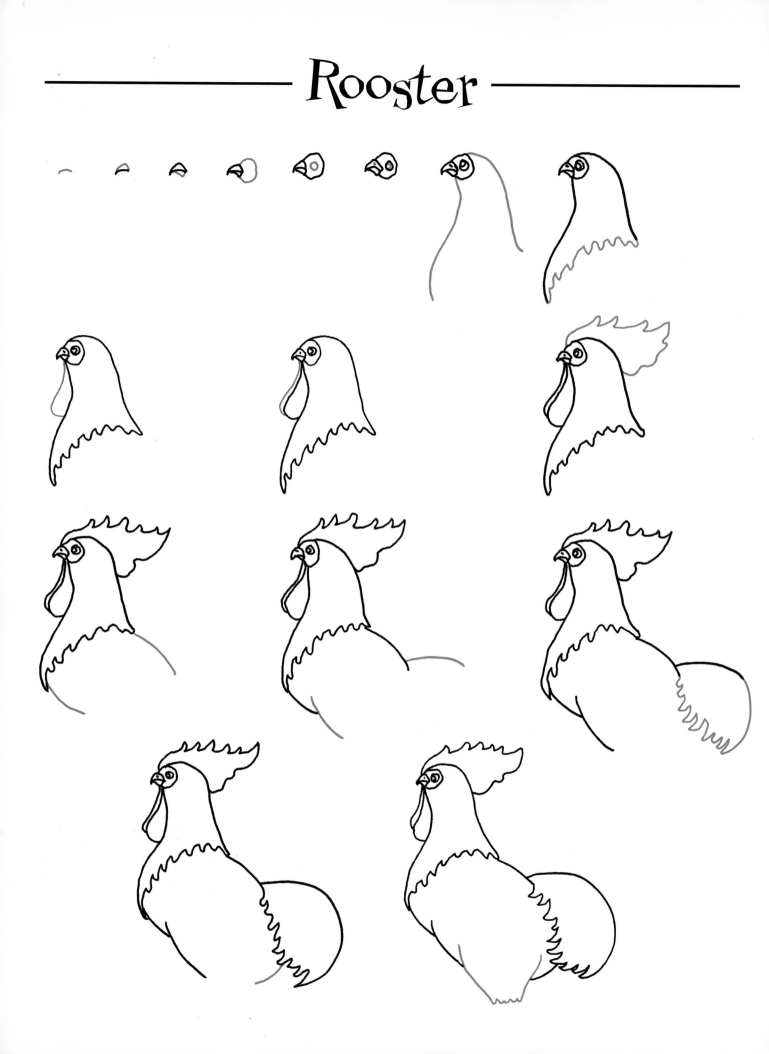

What clucky parents to have such cute chicks!

Try to overlap the shapes of the chicks.

crayon

Pig

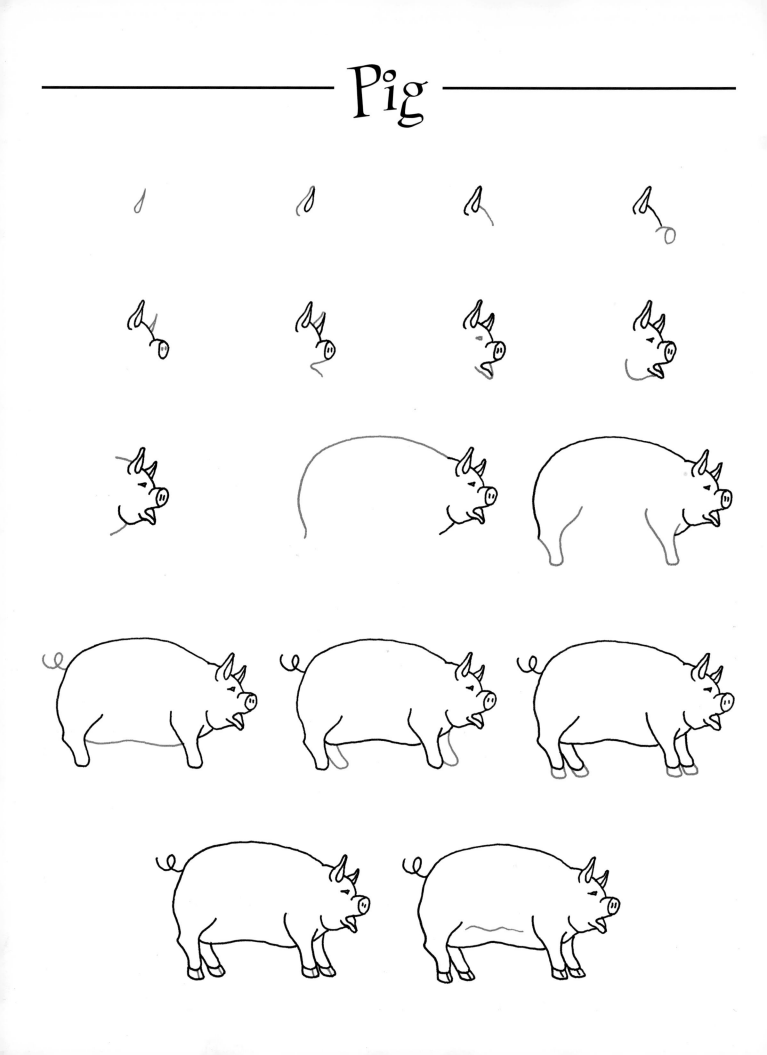

You're such a ham.

colored pencil

Grass and Hills

Billy Goat

This billy goat's not so gruff.

marker and pastel pencil

Flower (Daisy)

Dairy Cow

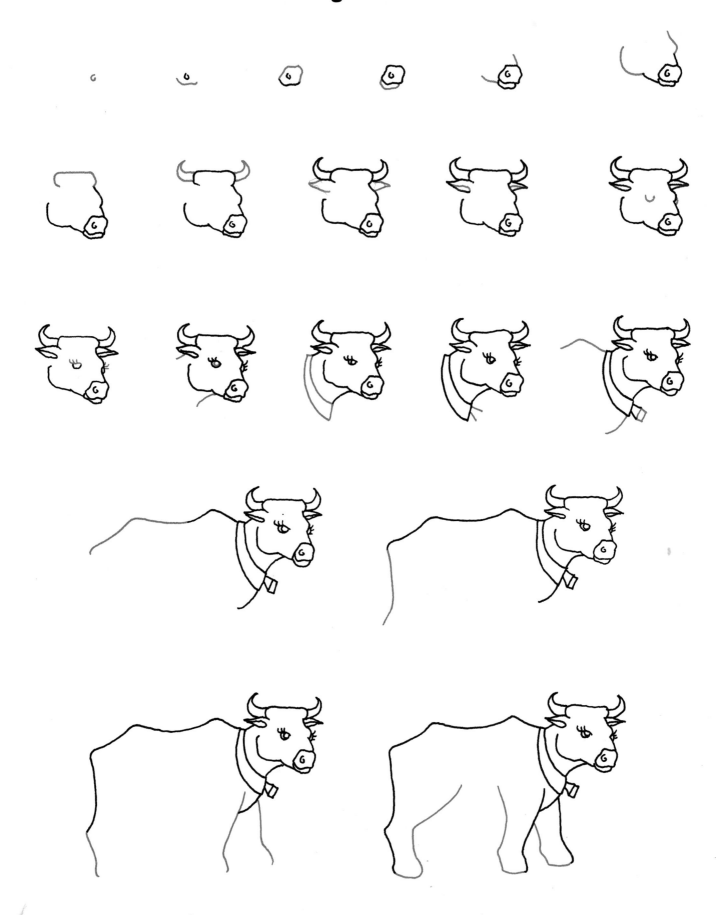

Stacked Hay Bales

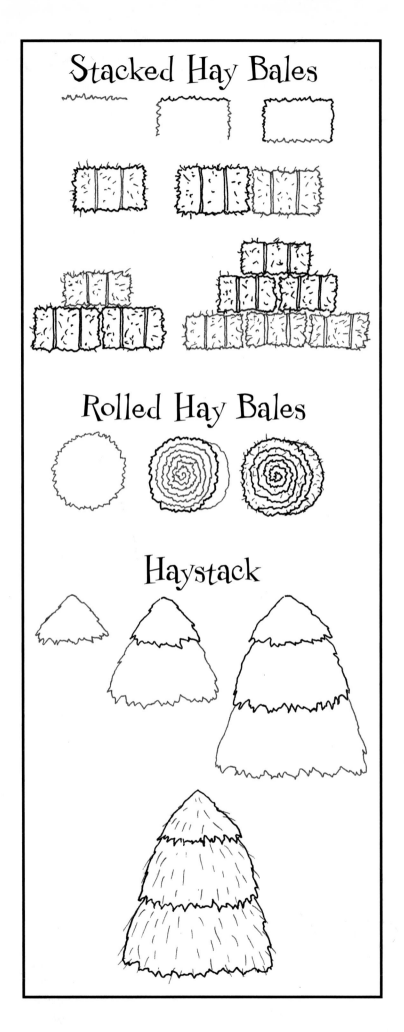

Rolled Hay Bales

Haystack

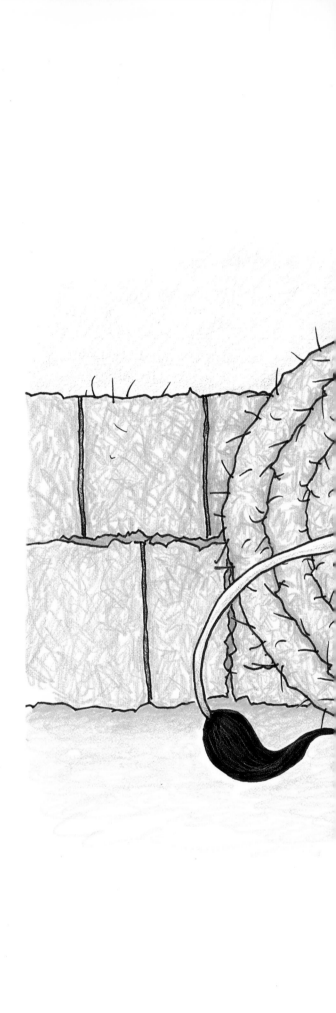

Hey! How about some hay?

marker and colored pencil

Horse

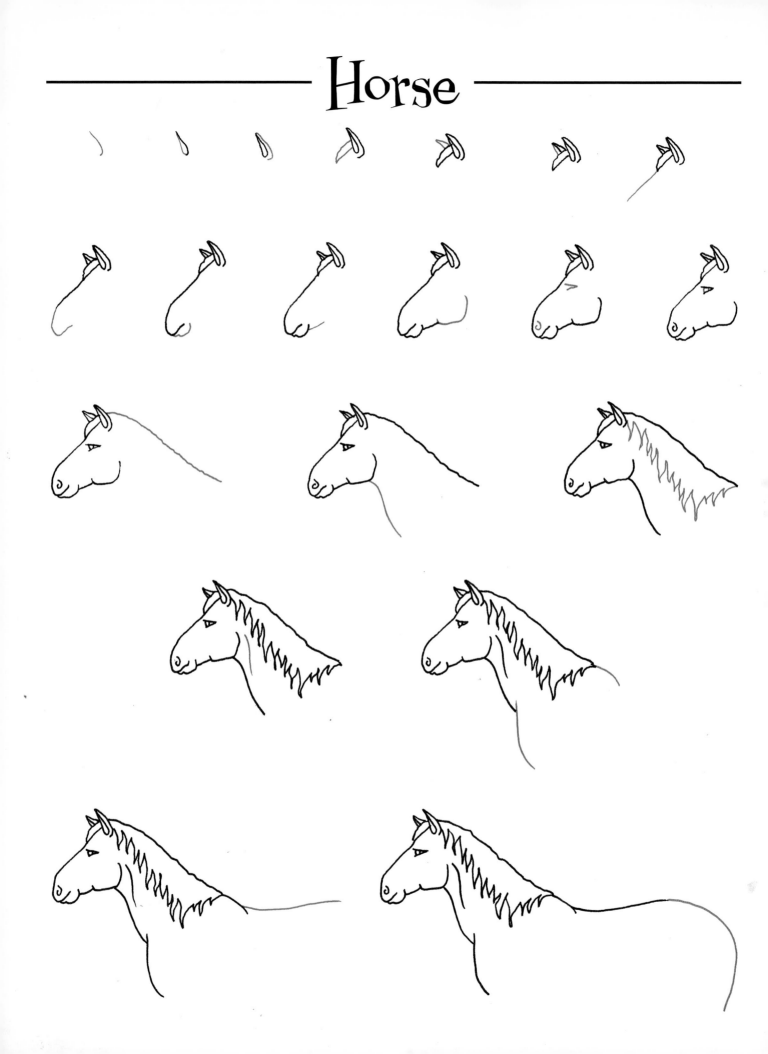

Put your best hoof forward!

marker and colored pencil

High-stepping Horse

Farmer and Tractor

Barn

Add a silo.

Add some bushes.

Add a fence.

Add some clouds.

And the sun.

And a welcoming road.

Old MacDonald drew a farm!